Osvaldo Golijov

T0081959

Demos Gracias

from *La Pasión Según San Marcos*

for SATB Chorus
and Two Percussionists

Playing Choral Score

HENDON MUSIC

BOOSEY&HAWKES

AN IMAGEM COMPANY

DISTRIBUTED BY

HAL•LEONARD®
CORPORATION
7777 W. BLUEMOUND RD. P.O. BOX 13819 MILWAUKEE, WI 53213

www.boosey.com
www.halleonard.com

Published by Hendon Music, Inc.,
a Boosey & Hawkes company
229 West 28th Street, 11th fl
New York NY 10001

www.boosey.com

First printed 2005
Second printing 2009
Third printing 2011
Fourth printing with Instrumentation page corrections, Nov. 2011
Fifth printing with dynamic changes in Perc., and final bar deletion, Nov. 15, 2011

TEXT

15. Demos Gracias al Señor

(Himno compuesto por fragmentos de los Salmos 113–118)
(Musica basada en el tema de la canción: Todavía Cantamos, compuesto por Víctor Heredia)

Coro:
Demos gracias al Señor
que su amor es eterno.
Demos gracias al Señor
y alabemos su nombre,
cantemos al Señor
que su amor es eterno
él es el Salvador.
Aunque tiemble la tierra
demos gracias al Señor
que su amor es eterno
él es el Salvador,
él reina allá en lo alto.

Cuando viene la muerte
y me enreda en sus lazos,
cuando me hallo preso
de miedo y dolor
y la angustia me alcanza
yo le canto al Señor.

Tiembla, tiembla tierra...

Aunque tiemble la tierra
y muerte viene a buscarme
yo te canto Señor
alabemos al Señor
cantamos, alabamos,
te damos las gracias Señor.

15. We Give Thanks

(Hymn composed from fragments of Psalms 113–118)
(Music based on a theme from the *canción* "Todavía Cantamos," by Víctor Heredia)

Chorus:
We give thanks unto the Lord;
because his mercy endureth forever.
We give thanks to the Lord
And glorify his name,
Praise we the Lord,
Whose goodness is eternal.
He is the Savior.
Even while the earth trembles
Give thanks to the Lord,
For his goodness is eternal.
He is the Savior
That reigns in Heaven.

When death comes and captures me,
And I am held in its noose,
When I am a prisoner
of fear and pain
and anguish touches me
I sing to the Lord.

Tremble, tremble, earth....

For though the earth trembles
And death comes to find me
I sing to the Lord
And give praise
to the Lord
We give thanks, O Lord.

PERCUSSION

1. Bombo drum

2. Spring Drum, Bombo drum

15. Demos Gracias al Señor

Variaciones sobre la melodia de la canción "Todavia Cantamos," compuesta per Victor Heredia

* These accents are just the natural culmination of the phrasing

** for instance, see 16–17, but extend the improvisation to *three* bars in mm. 22–24, and *four* bars in mm. 26-29

2

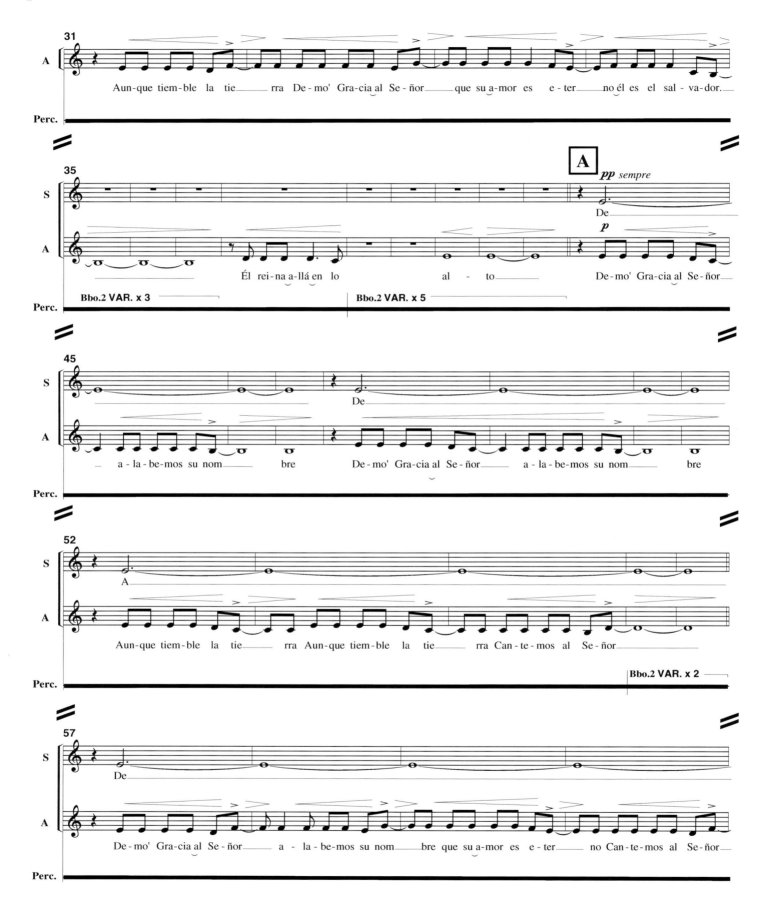

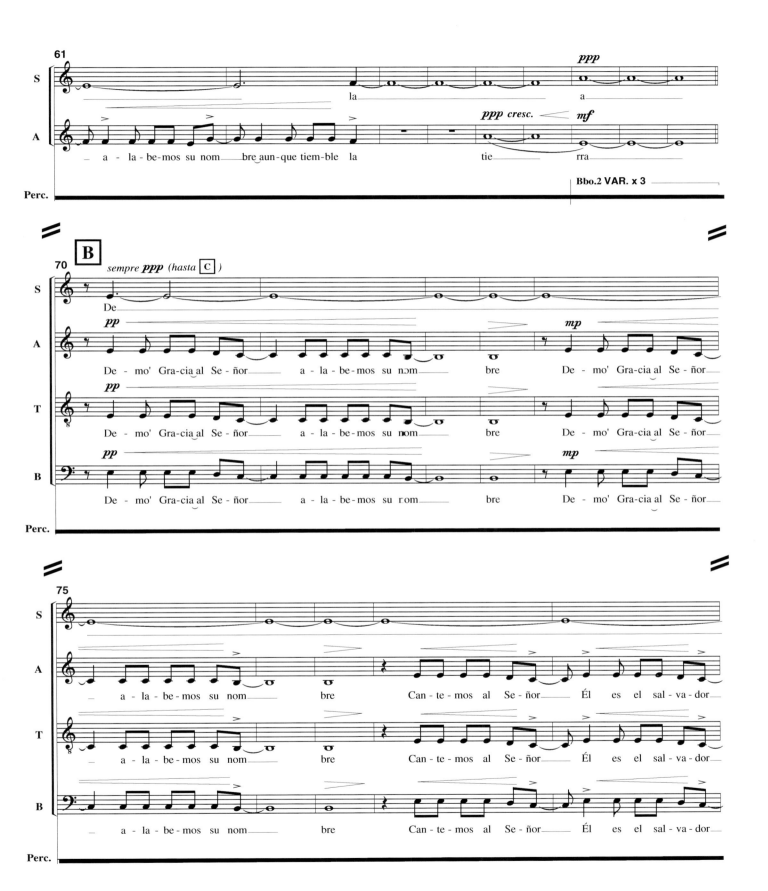

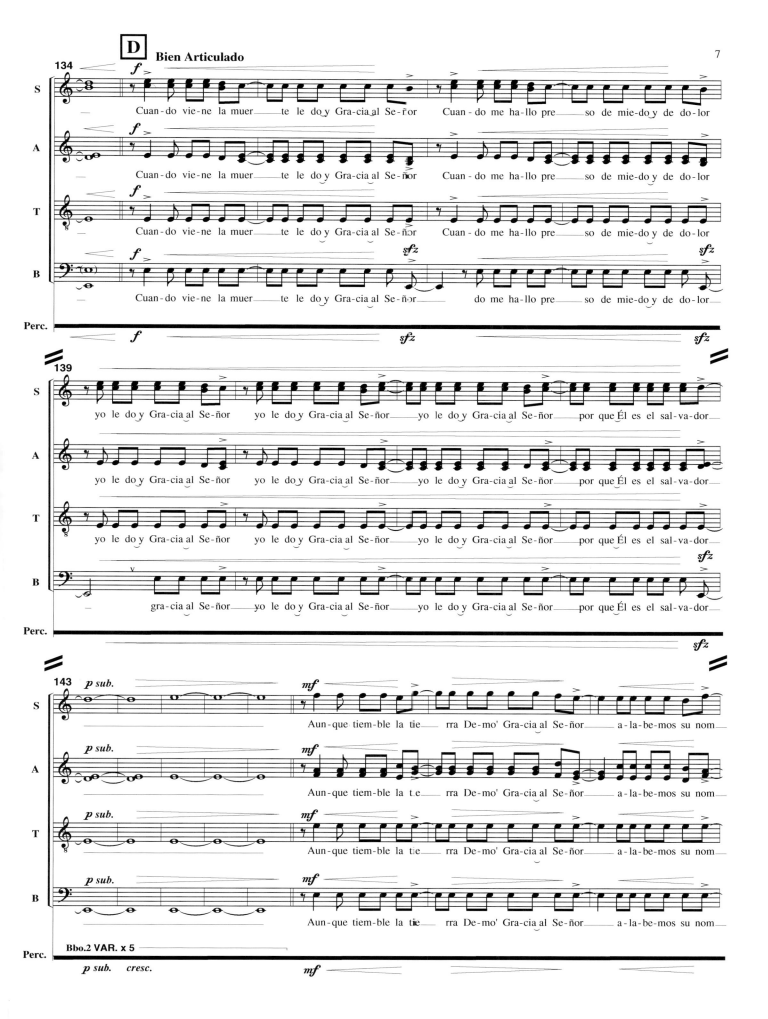

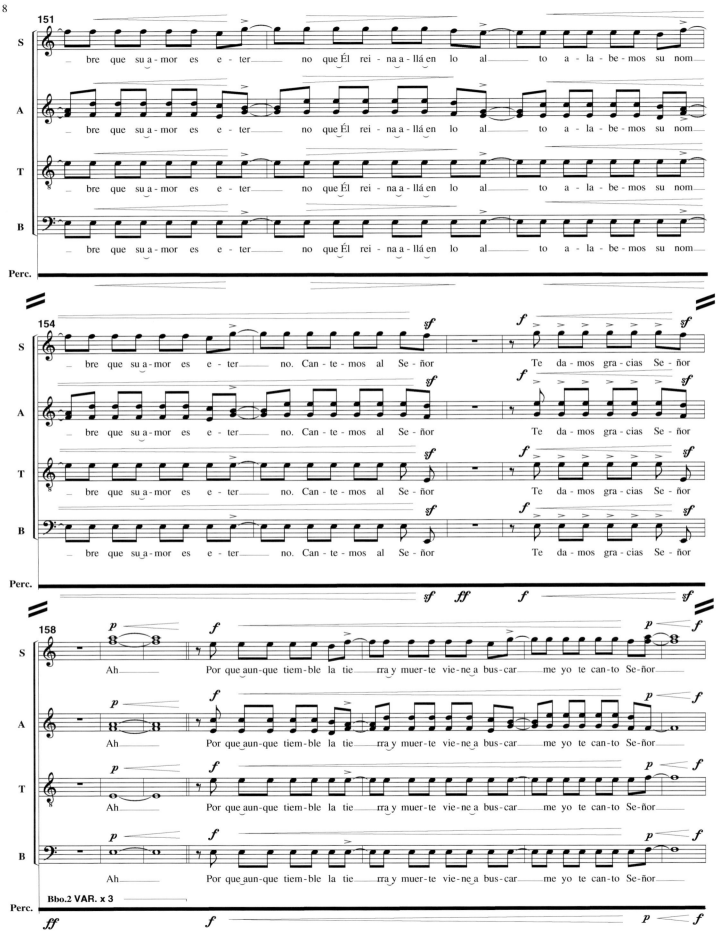

10

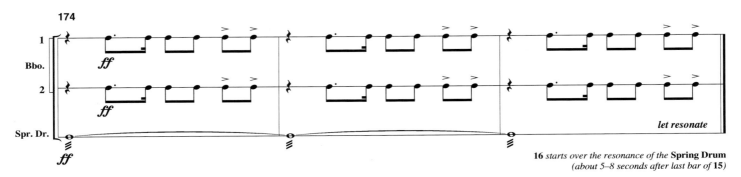

16 *starts over the resonance of the* **Spring Drum**
(about 5–8 seconds after last bar of **15***)*